Mr. Cornell's
DREAM BOXES

Jeanette Winter

Beach Lane Books

NEW YORK * LONDON * TORONTO * SYDNEY * NEW DELHI

If you had lived
on Utopia Parkway
not so long ago,

you might have walked past

this house.

You might have noticed
a light in the cellar window
and a moving shadow.

You might have seen Mr. Cornell
through that window,
working in the dim light.

Mr. Cornell didn't draw.
Mr. Cornell didn't paint.

Mr. Cornell made shadow boxes with things he found when he roamed the city—WONDERLANDS covered in glass.

Mr. Cornell wouldn't have noticed you looking in.

He saw mostly dreams and memories,
and he filled his boxes with them.

Mr. Cornell remembered watching the ball in penny arcades.

He remembered Coney Island Shoot the Chutes.

He remembered a dancer in the snow.

Mr. Cornell remembered blowing soap bubbles.

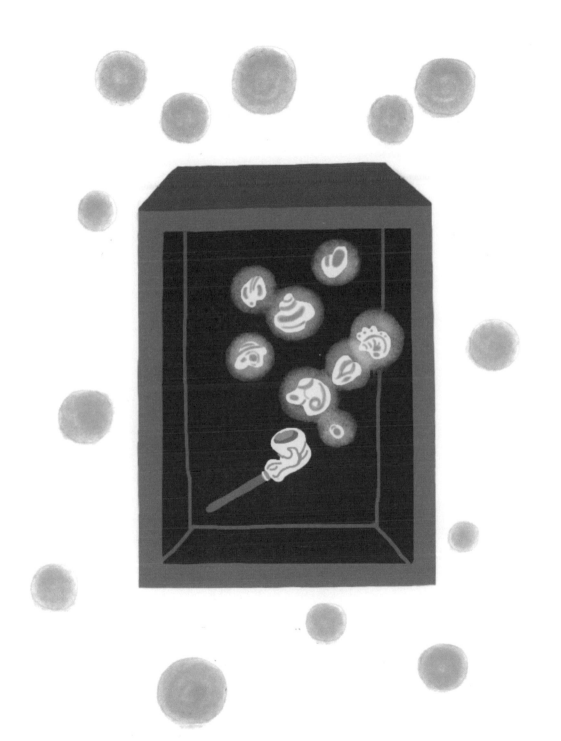

He remembered animals in the museum locked behind glass.

He remembered learning about stars,

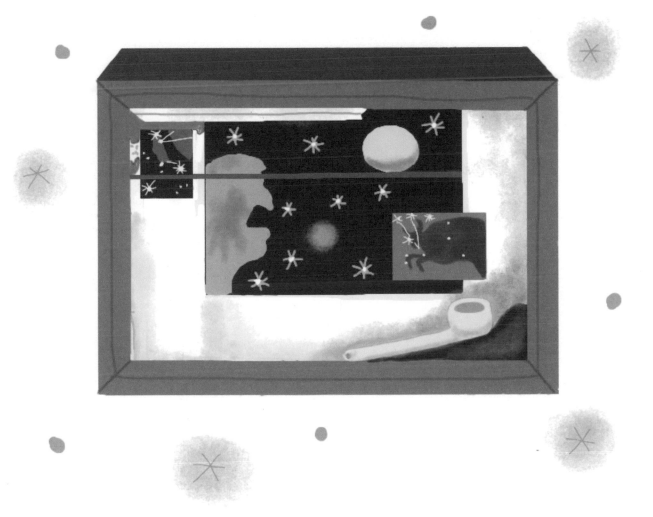

and how the endless sky scared him.

If the light in the cellar
was turned off,

you might have seen Mr. Cornell
sitting in his backyard
under a tree,

eyes closed,
dreaming.

He wrote about
his dreams,
and his thoughts,
and his ideas.

His journals filled
over 30,000 pages.

Remembering was important to Mr. Cornell.

If you looked at
the upstairs window,
you might have seen
Mr. Cornell
caring for his brother.

If the kitchen light
was turned on,

you might have seen
Mr. Cornell sitting at the
kitchen table, eating
a cupcake.

He loved sweets.

If you had lived on Utopia Parkway,
you might have opened your mailbox one day
and found an envelope addressed to you,

an invitation to an exhibition—
just for children—
of Mr. Cornell's dream boxes.

At the exhibition you would have seen Mr. Cornell

eating a brownie
and drinking cherry cola

and inviting

YOU...

to dream too.

JOSEPH CORNELL never studied art. He didn't paint or draw or sculpt. He was born in 1903, and he was a quiet boy. He lived in a house on Utopia Parkway in Queens, New York, until he died in 1972. In that house he looked after his mother, he cared for his brother, Robert, who had cerebral palsy, and he made magic boxes.

As Joseph Cornell crisscrossed New York City selling textiles to earn a living, he looked for old engravings at bookstalls and for objects that interested him. At home, he worked at the kitchen table, making collages with the engravings and making boxes filled with the objects he found. When the kitchen table was no longer big enough, he moved his work space to the basement.

Word of Joseph Cornell's boxes spread. Artists went to Utopia Parkway to meet him. Museums and collectors bought his work. He no longer had to sell textiles.

But children were Joseph Cornell's favorite audience. He sometimes even loaned his boxes to the neighborhood children. In 1972, the last exhibition Cornell attended before his death was held especially for children at the Cooper Union School of Art and Architecture in New York City. The boxes were hung three feet from the ground—child height. Usually reserved, Joseph Cornell was eager to tell children about his boxes and answer their questions.

From time to time, I make boxes too. I fill them with figures and shapes I cut out from tin and with things I have collected, like stones and mirrors. I like making these small worlds. Joseph Cornell was the master of the miniature magic world. This book is my tribute to him.

For Ann Bobco

BEACH LANE BOOKS

An imprint of Simon & Schuster Children's Publishing Division

1230 Avenue of the Americas, New York, New York 10020

Copyright © 2014 by Jeanette Winter

The photographs on pages 38–39 are from *A Joseph Cornell Album* by Dore Ashton

(Viking Press, 1974) and are reproduced with permission of the author.

BEACH LANE BOOKS is a trademark of Simon & Schuster, Inc.

For information about special discounts for bulk purchases, please contact Simon & Schuster

Special Sales at 1-866-506-1949 or business@simonandschuster.com.

The Simon & Schuster Speakers Bureau can bring authors to your live event. For more

information or to book an event, contact the Simon & Schuster Speakers Bureau at

1-866-248-3049 or visit our website at www.simonspeakers.com.

Book design by Ann Bobco

The text for this book is set in Grit Primer.

The illustrations for this book are rendered digitally.

Manufactured in China

0614 SCP

First Edition

10 9 8 7 6 5 4 3 2 1

Library of Congress Cataloging-in-Publication Data

Winter, Jeanette.

Mr. Cornell's Dream Boxes / Jeanette Winter. — First Edition.

pages cm

ISBN 978-1-4424-9900-3 (hardcover) — ISBN 978-1-4424-9902-7 (ebook)

1. Cornell, Joseph—Juvenile literature. I. Title.

N6537.C66W56 2014

709.2—dc23 • 2013020761

SELECTED BIBLIOGRAPHY

Ashton, Dore. *A Joseph Cornell Album*. New York: Viking Press, 1974.

Corman, Catherine, ed. *Joseph Cornell's Dreams*. Cambridge, MA: Exact Change, 2007.

Schaffner, Ingrid. *The Essential Joseph Cornell*. New York: Abrams, 2003.

Solomon, Deborah. *Utopia Parkway*. New York: Farrar, Straus & Giroux, 1997.

Summers, Joan, and Ascha Drake. *The Joseph Cornell Box*. Kennebunkport, ME: Cider Mill Press, 2006.